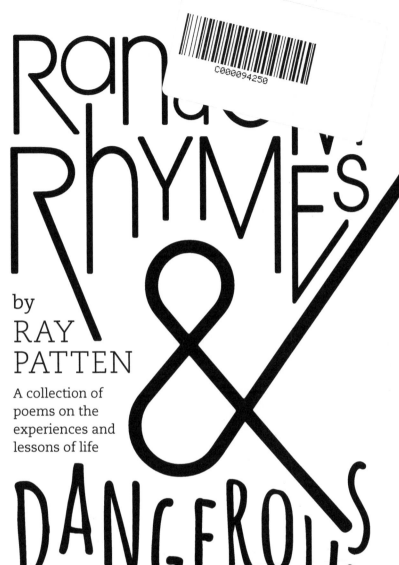

Random Rhymes &

by
RAY
PATTEN

A collection of
poems on the
experiences and
lessons of life

DANGEROUS
DOGGEREL

C000094250

First published in Great Britain as a softback original in 2021

Copyright © Ray Patten

The moral right of this author has been asserted.

Typeset in Sabon LT Std

Design, typesetting and publishing by UK Book Publishing

www.ukbookpublishing.com

ISBN: 978-1-914195-61-7

INTRODUCTION

These poems were written over a period of years and
were never originally envisaged to be put into print.

They have been performed and recited by me
at a number of venues such as open mic. events
to amuse and entertain those audiences.

Over the years I have frequently been asked
if the poems would be available as book.

Well, at last, here it is.

Having been written over a number of years,
several of the poems are a light hearted
reflection of what was happening at the time
and some are a trip down memory lane.

Others are simply my tongue in cheek observations
on the trials of life, whilst several are pure fiction.

I hope they will bring a smile to your face or
at least provide some food for thought.

Ray Patten

CONTENTS

Random Rhymes & Dangerous Doggerel

TO BALDLY GO

It's not much fun being bald
Not least of the problems is the names you are called
Like 'Baldy, 'Slaphead' 'Chromedome' and such
But I'm used to them now. They don't bother me - much

It's not as if I can help being bald
It happened and couldn't be prevented
When my follicle growth had permanently stalled
My self-esteem was quite seriously dented.

It's not 'cos my hair was abused or neglected
It was always kept neat and tidy
It was brushed and combed and always respected
And I washed it every Friday

I had a crew cut when I was a lad
That was the style back in the day
I didn't want to look like my dad
With his greasy Brylcreme DA

In the sixties the Beatle look had to be done
And I followed suit with the rest
Growing it out was rebellious fun
And mine was up there with the best

In the seventies the hippy look was hot
My hair grew longer as I got older
It grew and grew and believe it or not
It used to be down to my shoulder

But already the tell-tale signs were there
Though I was only about twenty
My forehead was higher, devoid of hair
In places where once there was plenty

Then a hole at the back made itself known
It was quite a shock to be honest
With the use of two mirrors, a pink spot was shown
Like a clearing in a forest

As time marched on my hair marched off
No longer a youthful mane
I could wash most of my scalp with a cloth
And I knew the instant it started to rain

Once I never had any hat to wear
Now the weather gives me good reason
What with the heat, the cold and no bloody hair
I need a hat for every season

The barber once said to me 'How would you like it?'
I said "Who are you trying to kid?
"I'll have a Mohican so wax it and spike it"
Now he just does the usual and charges ten quid.

It's a few minutes work and rather a joke
Which always strikes me as funny
That he can spend half an hour on some hairy bloke
But still charge me the same money

I've long since realized that life isn't fair
And it's really the luck of the draw
As to whether you keep or lose your hair
When you're older, or even before

The hairies may mock us from time to time
But we baldies must think on our feet
And always remind them of this telling line
- Grass never grows on a busy street

THE REFUGE

It's my favourite place of refuge
To escape from worry and woe
When it all just gets too much
It's down to the shed I go.

A little wooden building
That's only steps away
A place where time stands still
I can be in there all day

Dismantling bits of a motor bike
Or hacking bits of wood
Time spent in my shed
Always leaves me feeling good

I shut the door and the world outside
Can't interfere with me
Though it's only eight by six
In my shed I'm free

My mobile phone doesn't work in there
It really is a pain
But it's OK when I'm out of the shed
And turn it on again

Every bloke should have a shed
Doctors should prescribe them
The depressed and anxious would be cured
Just spending time inside them

There's always a job to be done in the shed
It never lets me down
So, sorry but I just don't have time for a
Shopping trip to town

There's nothing on the telly
Despite that we've got Sky
So I'm off to the shed again
'Till an hour or two's gone by

Is your mother coming round dear?
The thought fills me with dread
If you really, really need me dear
I'll be in the shed

Those things about your sister
I suppose I shouldn't have said
But you've said them yourself dear
You'll find me in the shed

Is it our anniversary dear?
I'd quite forgotten it.
Suddenly, it's crystal clear.
I'm really in the shed

ON THE BUS TO BRIGHTON

On the bus to Brighton
We shudder up Clayton Hill
Through the rain and steamy windows
We catch sight of Jack and Jill

Onward we pass through the Pylons
Which once were Brighton's gate
Now half bypassed stone built ghosts
Of the civic pride of '28

Past Patcham recreation ground
Cars parked in solid lines
Withdean is reached slowly
Amid a forest of traffic signs

Preston Manor stands shuttered
While on Preston Park's open green
An old man feeds the seagulls
So many he can barely be seen

Terracotta twisted fish
That once bore globes of glass
Now topped with disconnected wires
Look out on beds of weed and grass

Around he one-way system
And under the viaduct's span
I marvel at the achievements
Of the Victorians and their plan

Into Preston Circus
The fire station -1938
Still fulfils its purpose
And doesn't seem to date

Across the lights to London Road
With its pubs and charity shops
The bus pushes on through traffic
Fighting for space at the stops

The homeless in the doorways
The shop where credit's no trouble
Pity those who buy furniture there
And end up paying out double

Past St Peter's Church
Gloucester Place and Grand Parade
Though there's not much grand about it
These days I'm afraid

The Regency bow windowed houses
Though neglected are somebody's home
Blanket hung bed-sit windows
Stare blindly out at the Dome

Queen Victoria stands on her plinth
The Pavilion appears on the right
Locals pass by without turning their heads
While the tourists smile with delight

Old Steine traffic races around
Wheel less bikes are abandoned in chains
Brighton Pier beckons gleaming ahead
When only one bus stop remains.

We alight and walk to the seafront
To take in the view and the air
But are equally pleased and saddened
By the scene that greets us there

The i360 towers by the beach
Providing birds eye views of the city
While the skeletal West Pier just stands
Stark and forlorn, more's the pity.

The rusting sea front railings
Madeira Terrace's arches are closed
Shouldn't this heritage have been protected
Before anything new was proposed?

Brighton has such history and charm
But it's gradually fading away
So take the bus down to Brighton
And look for yourself someday.

BESOTTED

Didn't know where this was going
This thing with you and me
When I first met you not too long ago
I had a little drink with you
And then I couldn't see
That I would ever love and need you so

You went from meaning nothing
To being such a big romance
I think about you all through every day
Can't wait to get back with you now
Whenever there's a chance
And I don't give a damn what people say

I love your looks, your taste and smell,
You're there when I need you
You take me to where I can feel so free
My inhibitions all are gone
I have to say it's true
You know the very best and worst in me

My head spins when I'm with you
You make me lose my mind
I don't know how I'm ever gonna say
How I lived without you
Or how now I would find
My life without you every single day

But love and pain are always close
Sometimes the pain's too strong
My heart is aching and my mind confused
I know this has to end and
I know this must be wrong
I'm feeling kinda helpless and abused

We've had good times together
And I've loved you very well
But we have had our final run of luck
It's been a kind of heaven
And a kind of living hell
So booze, I'm gonna have to give you up.

THE REBEL

She's banned from her local pub
And her neighbours all seem to fear her
Although she can sometimes be friendly
There isn't much to endear her

She dresses in a most bizarre way
And her hair changes colour twice weekly
She's loud and brash and sometimes offensive
And does nothing at all discreetly

She drinks rather more than she ought to
And smokes a joint or two
She'll give any vice a try
There's nothing she wouldn't do

She likes to show off to everyone
Her piercings and her tattoos
And if you dare to look disapproving
She'll give you some verbal abuse

She'll say to you "I'll do what I like
What's it got to do with you?
I'm done with rules and convention
Now that I'm seventy two"

If her mother were alive today
She'd wish her daughter lived more tastefully
But she's a senior delinquent
Growing old disgracefully.

HEAVEN NOSE

I'm a fool for a girl with a nose
And what I mean is a big one
Not one of those
That's conventional, small and compact
Oh no, think more Cyrano De Bergerac

Be it Romanesque or perhaps aquiline
So long as it's a big one
By me it's just fine
To my mind there's nothing to make a girl cuter
Than a generously proportioned hooter

A nose with prominent angular line
So just one eye's visible
For most of the time
A nose that would really up the anti
With the likes of Streisand and Jimmy Durante

I'd swoon for a girl who had such a beak
So I'd instinctively duck
As she turned round to speak
And if she'd lie down facing North for a while
She'd come in quite handy as a sun dial

I'd plight her my troth whatever the cost is
Just so she could be mine
With her gorgeous proboscis
We'd live life in bliss doing things that excite us
And I'd feed her on garlic to ward off rhinitis

We would go to the pub so people could see
The vision of loveliness
Sitting with me
She say, "I must go off and powder my nose"
I'd say, "Be sure to get back before the pub's closed"

We'd live happy years together, we three
A ménage a trois
With herself, the nose and me
And when she expired, on her tombstone no doubt
Would be written these words 'Not
deceased, just conked out"

BLACK DOG

That old black dog comes around
And in my head he settles down
He brings the blues and I never can say
Just how long he's going to stay

And I say go home black dog
Just let me be
But that old black dog
Keeps following me

That old black dog sure gets me down
Makes me worry, makes me frown
Makes me drink, makes me sad
Makes me curse and makes me bad

Black dog, black dog, set me free
Take your blues away from me
Black dog, black dog, leave me alone
Don't gnaw at me like I'm your bone

That old black dog's been around for years
Bringing heartache pain and tears
When he's at your door don't let him in
He'll just keep coming back ag'in

That old black dog is a mangy stray
Kick him out, don't let him stay
Black dog will haunt you night day
You've gotta drive black dog away

So I say go home black dog
Just let me be
But that old black dog
Keeps following me

THE WEATHER FORECAST

I avidly watch the weather forecast
When it's showing on the TV
Is it sunny day or stormy blast?
I just have to watch and see.

Gone are the middle-aged gentlemen
Who once did the forecast so gravely
We'll not see those magnetic symbols again
Or hurricanes denied so bravely

Now we have carefully coiffured beauties
Who smile no matter what the weather will be
Undertaking their forecasting duties
Dressed more for a party, it seems to me

Or glib young men in smart suits and ties
Whose enthusiasm knows no constraining
With a backdrop of sunsets or leaden skies
To make the forecast seem more entertaining

The computer graphics whizz round on the screen
But we have to be patient and wait
While they tell us what the weather today *has* been
Just to bring us all up to date.

There are explanations of highs and lows
And of pressure systems building anew
Of which way and how strong the wind now blows
And what all that may mean for me and you

But then there's often some creeping doubt
That leaves me a little unsure
Should I take a mac and a brolly out?
Or leave a snow shovel by the door?

Will it clear up so I can mow the lawn?
And when will the rain finally stop?
I don't care if it's raining just around dawn
I'll be in bed then, not off to the shop.

There's more on the website I'm helpfully told
So I log on in anticipation
But the forecast there is several hours old
And merely adds to my frustration.

I don't bother checking what to expect
Of the weather a few days ahead
It'll almost certainly be incorrect
And contradict what was previously said

I'm not even sure why I want to know
What the forecast will be for the day
Be it rain, hail, or fog, sunshine or snow
I'll just have to endure it anyway.

So perhaps I won't bother to watch any more
I'll do something else instead
I'll get up in the morning and look out of the door
Or through the window from my bed!

WONDROUS WOOD

Have you ever stopped and wondered
If mankind ever could
Have evolved in the way that we have
If it weren't for wondrous wood?

Scientists say it's our language
And our opposable thumb
But without the wondrous wood
What would we have become?

From the very beginning it's been there
For man to use as he'd please
To create a civilisation
Wherever there were trees

Wondrous wood from trunks of trees
And wondrous wood from boughs
Wood for buildings, wood for boats
Wood for tools and ploughs

Wood to chop and chisel and saw
And shape to man's desire
And wondrous wood not least of all
As fuel for the fire

Wood of many different types
Each with its own special use
Oak and elm, willow and ash
Beech and chestnut and spruce

Plastics pose a threat to the world
But wood has a worth to the end
Bio degrading back into the earth
And remaining a lifelong friend

Wondrous wood we take for granted
Though its uses know no end
In our homes, in our work and daily lives
On wood we all depend

Our history is intertwined with wood
Just imagine life without it
So remember the value of wondrous wood
And never think to doubt it.

LEAVE ME ALONE

Leave me alone
Whatever you're selling I don't need it
Don't call me on the phone
Or send me brochure, I won't read it

Don't ring when I'm having my tea
I don't need covers for my chairs
Or a holiday, even if it's free
Nor a lift to get me up the stairs

Don't send me all your junk mail
I don't need a Zimmer just yet
My boiler's not going to fail
And I don't need to insure my pet

Don't tell me my computer is broken
And you can fix it from wherever you're from
I can tell from the moment you've spoken
That your name is not really John

Don't tell me I should write my will
I'll get around to it one day
I mean, I'm not even ill
I've no intention of passing away

Don't send all those damned emails
The ones that don't go to spam
Who gave you all my details?
How the hell do you know who I am?

Don't send those restaurant offers
With two main courses for one
There's not enough cash in the coffers
For a cup of tea and bun

Don't tell me that my double glazing
Is outdated and wasting my money
I don't care if your offer's amazing
Or that your adverts try to be funny

Don't tell me my gutters need cleaning
Or my drive would look nice done brick
Or my wheelie bin really needs steaming
And it can all be paid for on tick

Don't stuff all your take away menus
Through my front door every day
Stuff them all somewhere else
And leave me alone, I say

Don't tell me I should have done something
About my P.P.I.
And I don't want any box sets
From Virgin, Netflix or Sky

Don't tell me I'm paying too much
For the energy I use at home
Last time I changed my provider -
An hour and a half on the phone

Don't tell me that I should calm down
And really shouldn't take that tone
It was YOU who contacted ME, you clown
SO LEAVE ME ALONE

THE RELENTLESS TIDE

You can't see it
You can't touch it
You can't taste it
Or smell it

You can't own it
You can't hire it
You can buy it
But can't sell it

You can use it
You can lose it
You can count it
And waste it

You can pass it
You can find it
You can love it
Or hate it

It can fly
It can drag
It always goes
It cannot stay

It can beat you
It can cheat you
It can creep up
And run away

It's on your side
And it's against you
It's you enemy
And your friend

No matter what
You say or do
Time gets you
In the end

THE POWER OF ADVERTISING

There's no way to avoid adverts,
they're everywhere you go
They're in the papers, on the Internet,
on the telly and the radio
They try to tells us how to live, how
to think and what we need
They create our wants and desires,
and discontent and greed

They play on our emotions and try to win us over
If only we had this or that we'd live our lives in clover
But life is not like the adverts and their utopian ideal
If we really must have adverts why
can't they keep it real?

Chocolates delivered at midnight by
a mysterious man in black
Or was he just a sex pest who kept on coming back?
Chimpanzees to advertise tea made
animal lovers see red
So now we have a place in our hearts
for a knitted monkey instead

Instant mashed potato may have
been to the aliens' taste
But when I tried it years ago it was
more like wallpaper paste
Expensive creams and serums to iron out wrinkled faces
And stuff I don't want to know about
for rather more intimate places

Stock cubes that work wonders for
your dinner and family life
With an idyllic nuclear family
overseen by a dynamite wife
Vacuum cleaners with more suck
than you've ever had before
But still don't pick up quite every bit
of dust from off the floor

Stuff to throw in your washing machine
to make your clothes smell sweet,
Deodorants, soaps, and perfumes
for your body, head to feet
Gallons of it every day down the
drain and down the sink
So why is it so many people still continue to stink?

Sofas that are all always on sale to save you even more
And when it arrives the delivery guys
can't get it through your door
Some idiot shouting about kitchen
cleaner puzzles me I must confess
If he cleaned it a bit more often he
wouldn't have that mess.

Toys for kids that are supposed do
things that are quite fantastic
Are half the size you thought they'd
be, a forty quid lump of plastic
Supermarkets whose prices are
lower than they used to be
If everyone's cheaper than everyone
else, how come it isn't all free?

Cars that can race through snowfields
or up mountains without stopping
Which is all very well but hardly essential
if you only want to go shopping.
Shampoos and conditioners to make the
most unruly hair look perfect
Though looking around I'm not convinced
that you actually are all 'worth it.'

Penguins for gas, puppies for loo rolls
and Meer cats for insurance
Several times a night appear to test our
anthropomorphic endurance
Quick loans for when your boiler breaks
down and your cash has all been spent,
Don't concern yourself with the APR
of thirteen hundred percent

You can still get a loan with a guarantor
if your credit rating's poor
Then if you can't pay someone else
will. That's what friends are for.
Rest assured your deserted beach
holiday is fully ATOL backed
But don't expect compensation if your
tropical paradise is packed.

The unique CD collection that's not available in the shops
Which seems less of a bargain as
the first disc skips and hops
The operatic moustachioed buffoon
who appears from out of thin air
With a capacity to annoy me which
is way beyond compare

Nothing is quite what it appears in advert wonderland
Where reality is sanitized beneath the advertisers' hand
Where insight into our meagre
lives is but briefly glanced
Oh how those lives would be much
better, digitally enhanced.

So let us give praise to the advertisers
of our consumer society
Who feed our demands for goods
and services in infinite variety
Let us bow down to their superior minds
and their creative heads anoint
For *they* own the power of advertising,
the power to disappoint.

LET'S FACE IT

Cosmetic surgery's unregulated use
Really should be made unlawful
To put the brakes
On incompetent mistakes
That aim for awfully pretty
But end up pretty awful

AMERICAN AS A FOREIGN LANGUAGE

"Can I get a skinny latte?"
Asked the young man at the front of the queue
I was vainly hoping the reply would be
"Of course, it's a coffee shop
Coffee's what we do"

But "Certainly sir, - right away"
Was the response of the well trained barista
While wreathed in a cloud of steam
It seemed the young man found adding a "Please"
Just too hard a tongue twister

As he went to pay with a ten pound note
"Haven't got anything smaller have you?"
"Yes I have" or "No I haven't"
Was what I expected to hear
But instead I heard "Er -yeah I do"

The young woman dashed out from the meeting
And was really in quite a flap
"I'm making liver and bacon for dinner"
She'd got friends coming round but
I stopped myself saying
"Only cows, sheep and pigs can do that"

The newsreader said "The *Lootenant* was saved"
But his pronunciation tended to spoil it
In English we say *Leftennant*
To avoid confusion with a reference to
Someone who lives in a toilet

The "holidays" are not at Christmas
We don't go on "vacation" at all
We go on holiday in spring and summer
Or maybe skiing in winter or autumn
Which we do not call 'The Fall"

I don't have a cellphone in my pocket
Just a pay as you go mobile alas
Suspenders are really for women
But men here wear braces and put petrol in cars
We do not "fill up with gas"

A muffler to us is an old word for scarf
And a fender is found by the hearth
We wouldn't fix either onto our cars
Though tin cans and old boots are sometimes tied
To the bridegroom's car for a laugh

A sub is boat that that goes underwater
And a subway usually goes under a road
Sanders was of the river not a colonel
with a bargain bucket
And if you hear a croaking noise in the night
It's not a bullfrog, just a toad

Americanisation keeps creeping in
But there are other things just as bad
Like 'Could of" and Should of:"
And don't get me started on apostrophes
Their misuse just drives me quite mad!

THE FLEA MARKET

We enter in through church like doors
And wonder what this building used to be
With its high arched windows and creaky floors
Perhaps a school, a church hall, or a library?

Behind a counter from an old chemist's shop
A curmudgeonly figure sits reading the Sun
With nicotine stained glasses and flat cap on top
He glances suspiciously at everyone

A huge brass Victorian till to his right
Permanently showing two shillings and eight
Still keeps the cash all locked up tight
From the best deals he can negotiate

A chain of numbered cabinet keys
And a dog-eared book marked 'Bought and Sold'
Are under the counter down by his knees
And jealously guarded as though they were gold.

The stalls and cabinets create a maze
Of narrow aisles and dimly lit nooks
With carefully arranged displays
Of teetering china and things swinging on hooks

To some it's trash and to others it's treasure
Everything here can intrigue or amuse
Wander around and look at your leisure
Examine, inspect, ponder and peruse

Wallow in nostalgia at the kitchenalia
"We had a mincer just like that "
Wonder who wore the masonic regalia
Or who owned the battered silk opera hat

Old cameras, glass lampshades, and pictures galore
Cutlery, vases, cupboards and chairs
Jugs, cups and saucers and plates by the score
And there's even more of the same upstairs

Medals and coins and vintage fur coats,
Paperbacks, records and a two tone Dansette
Dinky toys, Hornby trains, models of boats
And a memorial plaque inscribed 'Lest We Forget'

A Silver Cross pram and a child's wooden scooter
Garden tools, well-loved teddys and china head dolls
A stringless fiddle and a curly brass hooter
A Jacques croquet set and some Henselite bowls.

A fireplace surround with art nouveau tiles
Candlesticks, handbags and a shrunken head
Old magazines in untidy plies
A doll's house, inkstands and a Put –U-Up bed

Black and white photos in an album all bound
With snaps of the seaside, perhaps some from abroad,
Show the simple pleasures they found
On their holiday trips in their pre-war Ford

Will our everyday items be equally treasured?
Will flea markets in future be easy to find?
Will the quality of our techno lives be measured?
By the material goods we leave behind?

The flea market's a brief glimpse into the past
But my memory's of something it doesn't sell
Though the things on display are varied and vast
What I always remember is – the smell!

WHAT IF

What if we had gender equality
In every possible way?
Not just in the obvious matters
Of equal rights and pay

What if everything else
Every gender stereotype
Disappeared from our daily lives
Almost overnight

What if he would rather talk
About relationships and how he's feeling
But she'd find discussing the football
Altogether more appealing

What if she had her mates round
For a game of cards and some beers
While he watched an old weepie movie
Alone, upstairs with his tears.

What if she always passed a mirror
Without glancing to check her looks
And he spent hours at the hairdressers
And collected cookery books

What if she thought it really funny
To belch loudly in front of his friends
Then bought him flowers from the petrol station
To say sorry and make amends

What if he wouldn't pick hair from the plughole
For fear of breaking his nails
What if she couldn't bear going shopping
And he couldn't wait for the sales

What if she kept a jacket and tie on
At work though the weather was hot
While he was barefoot in the office
In shorts and a low strappy top

What if she was out on her motorbike
With a noisy leather clad bunch
While he was alone in the kitchen
Preparing the Sunday lunch

What if the party invitation
Was met with howls of despair
And she was amazed when he cried out
"But I haven't a thing to wear"

What if she kept her phone in her pocket
And answered her calls straight away
While he kept his phone in his handbag
Where it buzzed unheard all day

What if she couldn't boil an egg
And seemed blind to household dirt
But he knows how to make a good soufflé
And can remove that stain from her skirt

What if he remembered the birthday
And anniversary cards they ought to send
What if she'd no idea of what's in fashion
And he's always really on trend

What if he has an awful headache
Sometimes on a Friday night
And he calls to her to remove from the bath
The spider that gave him a fright

What if we had more gender equality?
And what if we began to discover
That men and women might at last
Learn something from each other

THE MISTRESS

My mistress has a curvaceous figure
Much like her sisters', though they are all bigger
A long slender neck and a body so light
Her proportions from every angle delight

She dislikes the outdoors, a mystery to me
Because she was always attuned to the sea*   [*C]
But damp and cold she cannot endure
And would ruin her in the end, for sure

She's highly strung and can snap suddenly
When too much tension is caused by me
She has a sweet voice, which gladdens the ear
She can whisper seductively and speak out so clear

I spend many hours with her, hidden away
So others can't see us or hear us at play
I try hard to please her, late into the night
Until she lets me know I've done something right

She makes me fret, it's the way she is made
And gives no assistance to me, I'm afraid,
Of how to strike the right note with her
So that my intentions and hers can concur

If I mistreat her she'll squawk and protest
Although she knows I'm doing my best
I protect her and care for her, and when we are done
I make sure she is safe when I leave her alone

My mistress can be beautiful, really delightful
But also difficult, awkward and frightful
So I'm sure that by now you'll have solved this riddle
My mistress is no lady, she's just my old fiddle

SO YOU WANT TO COMPLAIN

So you want to complain
And why should you not
Get on the phone
While the issue's still hot

Kick up a fuss
Cause a stink, have a row
Make it quite clear
How you're feeling right now

Write a stiff letter
Tear 'em off a strip
Go give them hell
Give 'em some gyp

You don't have to put up with it
It really won't do
They've got realize
They're dealing with you

Spout off on Facebook
Or let rip on Twitter
Let them know that you're angry
Disappointed and bitter

Give them a lousy user review
There's a space on the website just for it
Write something damming, cutting and rude
So there's no way they can ignore it

Go in and see them
And bang on the table
Shout and swear at them
As much as you're able

Take some photos
Take someone's name
Then they'll know for sure
Just who's to blame

Demand an apology
And some compensation
For your time and trouble
Your pain and frustration

Write to your MP
(When you've found out their name)
Such an outrage as this
Mustn't happen again

Get the papers involved
The public should know
The injustice you've suffered
As the headlines will show

So you want to complain
Of course you do
Because nobody else
Is as perfect as you.

NOSTALGIA

When I see what's going on in the world
And how confusing life can become
I often think of my earlier years
Which I remember as so much fun

Didn't we have a better time
Back in the 'Good old days"
When life was straightforward and things were done
In easier simpler ways?

We all believed we knew where we stood
In ourselves and as a nation
There was never a doubt, no second thoughts
No ambiguity or complication

We had Winston Churchill,
Ovaltine, The Beatles and Ena Sharples,
Eric and Ernie, Norman Wisdom
MacMillan and Ernest Marples

Sunday night at the London Palladium,
Seaside holidays, Freddie and the Dreamers
Empty roads, no global warming
Compartment trains and Ford Cortinas

No one famous for just being famous
The GPO and BOAC
And on our black and white telly
Just the Beeb and ITV

Even granny knew what was number 1
In the top twenty hit parade
And we couldn't wait for those little brown packets
Every Friday when we were paid

Down the pub on a Saturday night
Church and roast beef on a Sunday
A mum always hoping for a nice dry day
For the washing every Monday

Omo for the clothes and Lifebuoy soap
Vim and Brobat bleach for the loos
The milkman delivered before it was light
Freeman, Hardy and Willis for your shoes

No central heating and only one fire
In the front room if we'd got some coal
We watched Cathy Come Home and learned about
The lives of those on the dole

We had the Cuban Missile crisis
John Profumo and Jeremy Thorpe
And saw the establishment start to crumble
But didn't give it too much thought

We were probably more concerned about
Whether our car would start in the morning
Would the radiator freeze, or would it break down
Halfway home without warning.

Anyway, we were alright then
We were British after all
We'd won the war, we were the best
And we couldn't possibly fall

We weren't concerned about equal rights
Or that prejudice was unjust and unfair
And as a white heterosexual male
Why would you even care?

Other countries national disasters
Raised little concern for our fellow man
Things like that didn't happen here
Until we had Aberfan

We didn't have Health and Safety
But we did have polio and whooping cough
We didn't know about smoking and cancer
Or that cholesterol could finish you off

So as we think back to days gone by
It is really quite plain to see
That when you take off the rose-tinted glasses
Nostalgia's not what it used to be.

PACKING UP

She's asleep in the other room
I'm quietly packing a suitcase
This relationship is doomed
A fact we both have to face

God knows we've tried
And talked when we weren't screaming
The love we had has died
To deny that is only dreaming

Into the case drips a lonely tear
As my angry thoughts turn to sad
And in my head I can only hear
"How did so good get so bad?"

The arguments have worn us out
That's why she's asleep in the chair
I can't even remember what it was about
But right now I don't really care

It's always something petty and small
That gets blown up out of all proportion
And we drive each other up the wall
With accusation and distortion

We know which buttons we have to press
To cause the most anguish and pain
We never learn from the previous mess
And we do it again and again

So it's come to this state of affairs
Now I'd rather live on my own
I put the case at the foot of the stairs
And glance around at what once was our home

It was a happy place 'till we ran out of luck
As the mantelpiece photographs show
But I'll have to tell her when she wakes up
She's bloody well got to go.

NEED WE SAY MORE?

A short biographical poem this is
On the life of Scott Joplin
- Rags to riches

ALL CHANGE

Dorothy Tanner was a lovely girl
Who was looking for someone to love her
A boyfriend, a soulmate, a fella, a chap,
A thrilling significant other

Sure, she'd had a few dates with men
From the factory where she was employed
But they didn't treat her as she would like
Or liked doing the things she enjoyed

Then one day a girlfriend at work said to her
"Would you like to try a blind date?"
"He's a friend of my cousin, a really nice man"
Desperate Dorothy just couldn't wait.

"Oh, tell me, what's he like? Do tell me more"
Dorothy was eager to know
"He works in the City, somewhere in the Square Mile"
"My cousin told me so"

So, the date was arranged for that Friday night
She'd meet him at Leicester Square station
She'd know the right man when she arrived
He'd be wearing a pink carnation

Dorothy ironed her pretty best frock
And made sure that her shoes were quite clean
With a squirt of her mother's eau-de-Cologne
She set off from Bethnal Green

Dorothy had not been up West too many times
So it was all exciting and new
She felt like a really modern young lady
Well, it was nineteen sixty two.

At Leicester Square she spotted the man
And she couldn't believe her eyes
He was tall and handsome with a military bearing
A most unexpected surprise

He introduced himself with almost a bow
Which Dorothy found to be thrilling
"Good evening Miss, I'm pleased to meet you,
My name is Alfred Shilling"

Dorothy held out her hand which he kissed
In a perfectly gentlemanly manner
"Good evening" she said as sweetly as she could
'And my name is Dorothy Tanner'

A moment elapsed before they both smiled
As their surnames began to sink in
"Fancy a Tanner dating a Shilling"
Dorothy blurted out without thinking

Alfred Shilling was the perfect gent
And Dorothy was over the moon
After a drink and the pictures, both agreed
They'd meet up again very soon

So they did and romance soon blossomed forth
As they dated evenings and weekends
It was quite clear to Dorothy and to Alfred
They were becoming much more than just friends

Alfred would insist that he always paid
For whatever their situation
Dorothy felt that she had struck lucky
To meet a man above her own station

One bright afternoon in Regent's Park
Alfred knelt down by Dorothy's side
And produced from his pocket a diamond ring
Which till then he'd been careful to hide

"Dorothy dear" Alfred said with a tremor
"I must ask if you would be willing"
"and agree to marry me as soon as you will
And become my own Mrs Shilling"

Dorothy would answer 'Yes" right away
But a question delayed her disposal
She said "Alfred there's one thing I must know,
"Before I reply to you kindly proposal"

"I know that you work in the City
And you seem quite well off it is true
But would you please tell me for my peace of mind
What exactly is it you do?"

Alfred stood up to his full height
And with his chest out but standing at ease
He proudly announced "I'm Inspector Shilling
Of the City of London Police"

"It's a steady and respectable job
With good pay and a pension too
We can make a good life Dorothy dear
A bright future for both me and you"

Dorothy's face fell, she looked quite aghast
Her dreams had all come a cropper
"I can't marry you Alfred" she said with tear
You may be a Shilling, but you're really only a Copper

STUMBLE ON

The road is rocky to where I'm bound
The only way that I have found
Can't turn back, there's no return
There's been some lessons learned

Pushing on through storm and rain
Aching, tired and full of pain
There's no horizon I can see
On the highway back to me

But I stumble on,
I stumble on,
I must be strong
When hope is gone,
I stumble on.

Scared to go back where I've been
And see the things that I have seen
Thought that I was having fun
But can't believe the things I've done

Sometimes it's dark and I can't see
The way that things once used to be
Faded memories in my head
Light the bumpy road ahead

When this road comes to and end
I pray that I will find again
The man that I once used to be
And live my life just being me

But I stumble on,
I stumble on,
I must be strong
When hope is gone,
I stumble on.

THE FORLORN OAK

The old oak still stands after all these years
Its glory now lost in its skeletal remains
What history and stories of joys and fears
The ancient wood itself contains

Its once strong branches, now white and bare
Are gaunt and without bud or leaf
And yet the truth of its life is there
A life from which it now knows relief

In early days it grew strong and robust
Knowing the tests and trials it would meet
It resolved to develop, adapt and adjust
To meet every challenge and roundly defeat

It stood tall, alone, secure and tough
To weather storms, drought, ice and snow
To prove itself always strong enough
And its own suffering never thought to show

But never did it live for itself alone
Many other lives so tirelessly supported
In the lee of its branches have their lives known
Of its shelter, nurture and comfort undaunted

The embracing ivy that constantly clung on it
The creatures and birds that depended upon it
The children that played and climbed and swung on it
The generations of saplings whose lives sprang from it

The oak's life is over but though forlorn and neglected
The legacy of its strength and shelter and giving
Should always be honoured, remembered and respected
A lesson to mankind in the art of living

WE'VE DONE IT ALL BEFORE

Some people think we're out of
touch, just because we're old
But that just shows they don't know
much. Our story must be told
We were young and had our day and set the world alight
We raised hell along the way and made our mark alright

Sex and drugs and rock and roll
and love and peace and war
Is nothing new I'm telling you, we've done it all before

Teds and rockers, mods and punks, everything was new
We broke the mould and trashed the
rules. We paved the way for you
To stop the war in Vietnam we
met in Grosevenor Square
And went to San Francisco wearing flowers in our hair

We were there in Hyde Park to see the Rolling Stones
When Jagger spoke we shed a tear
for the loss of Brian Jones
We were at the Isle of Wight and tore the fences down
Slept rough in Brighton overnight
for a battle in that town

Our music came from Caroline broadcast from the sea
And forced a change of attitude from Aunty BBC
That music does not fade away
though half a century's gone
You'll still hear it every day. The beat goes on and on.

Beads and kaftans, summer of
love, pot and sex and Hair
It's said if you remember it, you really were not there
We railed against convention and
changed the world of fashion
We found a shared intention and
pursued it with a passion

We pushed our parents to the brink
just like you do yours
We were wilder than you think and
all in the same lost cause
Our legacy we freely give but
there's one thing we expect
Don't write us off or put us down,
please show us some respect!

Because sex and drugs and rock and
roll and love and peace and war
Is nothing new I'm telling you, we've done it all before

STUFF

It seems to me that nowadays
We've all got too much stuff
It's all must haves and essentials
And too much is never enough

Gotta have this, gotta have that
More from want than need
Order, buy, click and collect
Fulfil your need for greed

Wave your card at the little machine
And ping it's yours in a flash
How much more painless it feels
Than parting with cold hard cash

Irresistible bargains that save you a mint
You lug home feeling smug and proud
Until you admit that though it was cheap
It's something you could've done without

Our houses are cluttered with all this stuff
There's not a cupboard, shelf or drawer
That's not packed to capacity, groaning and creaking
Not an inch to take anything more

All those books you've read just the once
And never likely to read again
On show on the shelf to convince everyone else
That you've an educated brain

The frock you bought for somebody's wedding
That's not since seen the light of day
Probably doesn't even fit you now
But you can't bear to give it away

All those kitchen gadgets
To make your cooking cordon blue
Worked wonders in the advert
But wouldn't work for you

Your old mobile phones and the boxes they came in
Are obsolete, useless, and charge less
But they cost you so much when they were new
You still store them away regardless

Half rolls of wallpaper, odd bits of wood
Things you'll never get around to mending,
Old birthday cards, unwanted presents
The list is never ending

"Our house is too small, we'd like to move
To a little bit bigger place"
But bet your life in year or two,
They still haven't got enough space.

We are ruled by stuff and the acquisition of
The material things we desire
When in truth it really wouldn't matter
If we threw most of it on the fire

Stuff takes up our time, space and money
It can drive us to bankruptcy and drink
Inanimate objects stuff may be
But they're more dangerous than you'd think

So as you go through life
Whatever you do
Get control of your stuff
Before your stuff stuffs you.

THE MAN OF THE HOUR

Harold was not the most amorous lover
But his girlfriend said she'd like to believe
There'd be bells and fireworks
when they loved each other
So he bedded her at Midnight on New Year's Eve.

SOME CAREERS ADVICE

Work as an antique dealer
Is really nothing new
But becoming a radiologist
Would clearly see you through

The trainee pilot's programme
Hasn't taken off quite yet
And life as a professional gambler
Is probably not a good bet

Some of the plumber's regular work
Sends them round the bend alas
But the chef's career can often be
Really cooking on gas

A professional skier's career
Can only go downhill
But solicitors are often found
Working with a Will

Steeplejacks climb the ladder
To keep their wages up
Pet shop owners are only too pleased
To be literally sold a pup

Sunflower growers never mind
If their work all goes to seed
Cannabis growers are just the same
When their crop turns into weed

Bakers working overtime
Really knead* the dough   [*need]
But manufacturing sat navs
Could be the way to go

A golfer's way of living
Is sure to be full of holes
And professional footballers often find
They don't quite reach their goals

Musicians do their best and try
To achieve a career of note
But there's something about a voice coach
That just sticks in my throat

Comedians do it for a laugh
But jokes sometimes fall flat
Cricketers can further their careers
Entirely off their own bat

Dog walkers are always looking
For just a few more leads
Conveyancers certainly don't believe that
Words speak louder than deeds

Milliners luckily have a job
That always goes on ahead
Whilst a tailor's work always seams*   [*seems}
To have a common thread

Working as a farmer
You reap just what you sow
And working with radiation
Might give you a bit of a glow

There are very many elements
To a chemist's job these days
Whilst lift attendants stand at the door
Hoping for a raise

Palaeontologists make no bones
About the work they do
And tyre fitters always seem
To be well rounded too

Train drivers usually have their careers
Going along the right lines
And horologists work to make quite sure
They keep up with the times

Mattress manufacturers
Don't take it lying down
And circus performers are the only people
Paid for acting the clown

Cobblers give their awl* at last   [*all]
Even if they're down at heel
Though film producers sometimes think
Their work is not for reel*   [*real]

Working as a white line painter
Is middle of the road
Whilst being a lorry driver
Will affect your working load

Fishing for a living
May well get you hooked
And becoming a librarian
Will keep you fully booked

People who make parachutes
Will always let you down
But in a café serving breakfast
You'll be the toast of the town

If you want to work with money
In large or small amounts
The place to go, I'm sure you know
Is a bank, by all accounts

Working on a funfair
You'll be travelling roundabout
But putting up public exit signs
You'll always be on the way out

A taxi driver's work is fare*   [*fair]
Butchers can get the chop
And the lollipop lady's daily job
Simply has to stop

The dentist really knows the drill
The carpenter's had his chips
The auctioneer's hammered every day
And nurses keep dealing with drips

Recording a Top Ten hit single
Wouldn't be amiss
But what about being a urologist?
Would you really be taking- advantage?

THIS TENNIS RACKET

I took up tennis late in life
For a bit of exercise
Nothing too strenuous you understand
At my age it seemed only wise

I took some lessons and was so pleased
When I finally managed to get,
After many attempts in several sessions,
The ball back over the net

Backhand, forehand, serve and volley
All defeated me time and again
But after while I managed a smile
When my racquet connected with my brain

So I joined a club and went to play
With some others I'd got to know
For a couple of hours on Friday evening
Then off to the pub we'd go

The laughs we'd have as we did our best
To play better each week than before
The arguments we'd have for minutes on end
When no one remembered the score

"It's thirty fifteen" one would say
"No, forty fifteen on the right"
"Let's call it thirty all" I'd suggest
"Or we'll be here all bloody night"

We applauded ourselves for rallies
If they were only six shots or so
No one could ever serve an ace
If they did we'd ask them to go

We'd book our court a week in advance
And look forward to playing again
Only to find that on Friday night
Inevitably It would rain

As the years have gone by we have all improved
And the play can become quite intense
But it can be frustrating to keep players waiting
When our balls get stuck in the fence

THE CIRCLE OF FIFTHS

If you want to play a musical instrument
Sooner or later you'll need to know this
It's a little circular diagram
Which is called the Circle of Fifths

It's a circle divided up like a clock
With twelve segments on its face
And in every segment all major and minor
Keys have their appropriate place.

So let's start at the top with the easy bit
And there is the key of C
With no sharps or flats, just natural notes
It's as simple as can be

Also up there is what is called
The major keys relative minor
Which in this case is A, at three notes below
Being the minor's constant definer.

Moving round clockwise to one o clock
We come, not as you may think, to D
But because we are moving on in fifths
The next key that we come to is G

This the first key that has a sharp note
Which it shares with its minor of E
That note is F sharp which must always be played
If you're playing a tune in G

As we move round to two o clock
We add one more sharp to the key
The sharp is C in the major key D
And the relative minor is B

Now it starts to get tricky as we get to three
Going up a fifth we come to A
Where we add a G sharp to the other two sharps
And for the minor it's F sharp we say

Now we're round down at four o' clock
And we arrive at the key of E
A fourth sharp is added, and it's D this time
And the minor is C sharp, you see.

By five o clock the lines of the stave
Are quite cluttered as we add a sharp A
To the key of B major or G sharp minor
When it's five sharps we now have to play

At six we find F sharp major, E flat minor
D sharp minor and also a major G flat
Now with six sharps or six flats I strongly suggest
You keep well away from all that

At seven it's even more complicated
With D flat and C sharp major keys
B flat and A sharp minors as well
With *seven* sharps or flats if you please

At eight we move into the flat keys
With A flat major and F minor too
And flats of B, E, A and D
Which spells Bead to help remind you

At nine o clock we're into E flat
And it's getting simpler for me
We knock off the D flat to leave B, E and A
With the relative minor of C

At ten it's B flat and also G minor
With only two flats left
We remove the A and keep B and E
The only flats next to the clef

By eleven we are on easy street
With F flat major with just a flat B
Which brings us back to the start
At twelve o clock with C

It may take a while to grasp all of that
So you could take a tip from me
If you want an easy musical life
Play everything in C or G

AIDE MEMOIRE

My wife says I'm getting forgetful
And my memory's becoming quite poor
She says it's a bit of worry that she
Can't rely on me any more

Well yes, I'm getting on a bit
And I've a lot to remember these days
So it's not surprising that now and then
Some things are a bit of a haze

All those years of information
That have been absorbed by my brain
Filed away at the back somewhere
Struggle to come to the front again

All those terabytes of data
And no search engine to find any fact
But I'm meant to recall things from years ago
At a drop of the proverbial hat

What she wore when we went to pictures
And saw that film starring whatshisname
And which of her favourite shoes were ruined
When her heel got caught in a drain

Long deceased relatives I never knew
Peoples' phone numbers and names
When and where those photos were taken
Or how much we paid for the frames

What so and so said to thingumabob
Donkey's years ago
Apparently it was so shocking
She can't believe that I really don't know

Which of her clothes wash at thirty degrees
And what things must be washed on hot
Which things must be ironed using a cloth
And some inside out and some not

The name of restaurant, long since closed
Where we went on our first date
The colour of the tablecloth, the name of the waiter
What it cost and what she ate

Apparently more recent things
Can tend to slip my mind too
Like pin codes and passwords and date on which
Her next hairdressing appointment is due

So now I have the answer
So she'll no longer tut and frown
I've got a secret little notebook
Where I've jotted everything down

It's got all the facts
And I'll find what I want with just a sneaky look
My memory's reputation redeemed
With my trusty little book

My constant companion
My memory's salvation, I'll take it wherever I go
Though where the hell I've put it
I'm buggered if I know.

THE SEASONS TURNAROUND

Summer now is over
And autumn's under way
The sun sinks slowly lower
And shortens every day

The winds rise up
The temperature's down
The green all disappears
As the leaves turn brown

The once welcome rain
Now becomes a curse
While the weather forecast
Gets steadily worse

Soon the clocks go back
And the heating goes on
Winter arrives
And remains for too long

The darkness, the cold,
The rain and the snow
Staying indoors
Nowhere to go

Leaves on the line
Essential workers on strike
Scraping ice off the car
Getting soaked on my bike

No more swimming in the sea
Or sunbathing on the sand
Get out the coats and jumpers
And keep the Beecham's to hand

No more garden parties
Or weekend barbeques
Your sunshade and your deckchairs
Will be of no further use

What with all of the misery
That winter's bound to bring
I'm just going to hibernate
Wake me up in the Spring

I can then avoid Christmas
Bah humbug, that'll be me
Artificial merriment
Around the artificial tree

Sending cards to people
I haven't seen for years
The in laws round all Christmas day
Boring me to tears

Trying hard to look so pleased
With the awful presents they bring
No thanks. I'll pass on Christmas
Wake me up in the Spring

Mind you, I do have a drink or two
When in the in laws have gone away
I quietly drown my sorrows
For the whole of Boxing Day

Then of course there's New Year too
Another good excuse
To forget all the health advice
And enjoy some jolly good booze

Closely followed by Burns' Night
When the haggis goes to slaughter
And we get slaughtered much the same
As the whiskey flows like water

And what about the cosy nights
Beside the blazing hearth
At the local pub, with your mates
For more drinks and a laugh

Soon enough it's St Patrick's Night
Another fine cause for a drink
You can try to keep count but bet your life
You'll have had more than you think

So now I'm having second thoughts
And my doubts have all been quashed
I'll get through winter easily enough
Permanently sloshed.

WHERE IS THE SNOW?

We're getting ready for Christmas
Can't wait for the day to come
We've got the tree and the turkey
It ought to be lots of fun

We've got everyone a present
So we're all set to go
Except there's one thing missing
We ain't got any snow

Where is the snow?
Where is the snow?
We pray for snow but snow don't show
Ain't had no snow since we don't know
Somebody bring us some snow

Snow on all the Christmas cards
And every TV ad.
We need some snow at Christmas
To stop us feeling bad

We used to get snow at Christmas
If it only lasted a day
We don't get snow at Christmas now
The snowman's gone away

We've been to lots of parties
And often we have found
Even if the weather's nice
There's lots of snow around

We'll bet there's snow in Hollywood
And all those lovely places
Where people really like the snow
You can see it on their faces

We can't get snow in any
Of the high street shops you know
Though they say every little helps
They can't sell us any snow

We can't get snow on line at all
No matter how much dough
We clock up on the credit card
We can't buy any snow

We don't like cold turkey
But we'll be having it again
We've got some artificial snow
But it isn't quite the same

When we look out for nice white snow
All we get is green grass
There is no snowy wonderland
Through our old looking glass

Where is the snow?
Where is the snow?
We pray for snow but snow don't show
Ain't had no snow since we don't know
Somebody bring us some snow

So Santa if you're listening
To our tale of woe
Be nice to us this Christmas
And send us all some snow

We hope that you all get some snow
To make your Christmas day
And if you find there's some to spare
Please send a bit our way.

NOTHING TO DO
(ON THE OUTBREAK OF CORONAVIRUS)

I can't go out
I've no reason to
So I'm here at home
With nothing to do

The Government said
Reduce social contact
I heard their advice
And had to react.

I got in a bit of shopping
But didn't panic buy
Lots of people did, though
I couldn't see quite why

I'd like to go the pub
Or out for a meal somewhere
But I'm told that's all too dangerous
I really must take care

So here I am, stuck home
The prospects look quite bleak
Already run out of things to do
And it's only been a week

I've done that bit of decorating
And my cupboards are all tidy
I've cleaned the house from top to bottom
And still it's only Friday

I've emailed my friends and they're all OK
Although they're dreading the thought
Of the kids being at home all day
And no theatres, no cinema, no sport

I've already read my library book
And now can't get another
I've posted off a Mother's Day Card
Because I can't go and visit my mother

My diary is full of crossings out
As events and meetings are cancelled
My social life is being slowly
Systematically dismantled

My busy life has slowed right down
In only a week or two
Not long ago I often thought
It would be nice to have nothing to do.

THE COVID PUB CRAWL
(AFTER THE END OF THE FIRST LOCKDOWN)

When the Government said we could go to the pub
After lockdown, that was good to know
With a mask and plastic gloves in my pocket
I got myself ready to go

Like everyone else I'd not had a pint
At a pub or a bar since goodness know when
So off to the local with great anticipation
For a lovely, long, cold beer once again

I walked along briskly, no time to waste
'Till a sign in the window disclosed
"The landlord is shielding from Covid 19
So this pub is regrettably closed"

Undeterred I went on in my quest for a drink
To a bar that I knew quite nearby
A short while later I saw that was closed too
But there was no indication as to why.

Getting thirstier now from my lengthening hike
I walked on to the next pub in town
Only to find it was all boarded up
With sign simply saying, 'Closed down"

Just then the rain started but I didn't give up
Though like a drowned rat I must have looked
When I got to the next bar the doorman just said
"You can't come in if you haven't booked"

'I've got to be lucky this time" I thought
As I mooched towards pub number four
But that was closed too and passerby said
"The brewery's not working no more"

As darkness drew in I could see some light
From a place that I knew opened late
Then I saw on the door much the same as before
"Closed while our staff isolate"

Onward I slogged on my self-imposed quest
Until the next pub came into view
On a rain splattered blackboard I barely discerned
"Staff shortages. Closing at Two"

Then I remembered a pub that had been there for years
But as I rounded the corner then that's
When I saw the old place had been knocked down
And was being developed for flats

Now I thought I'd struck lucky
When I spotted bar number eight
But the man on the door said "There's no room for more"
"You'll have to stand outside and wait"

So I stood in the rain to wait for a space
And couldn't believe it when
Everyone came out and the doorman said
"Sorry mate, we now close at ten"

So I had to resort to a convenience store
To buy a six pack of booze
And trudge back home to my own front door
To drink to my 'Eight Bar Blues'

BV - #0018 - 181121 - C0 - 203/127/5 - PB - 9781914195617 - Gloss Lamination